Original title:
Quips Among the Quaking Aspen

Copyright © 2025 Creative Arts Management OÜ
All rights reserved.

Author: Finn Donovan
ISBN HARDBACK: 978-1-80567-386-6
ISBN PAPERBACK: 978-1-80567-685-0

Jive of the Sun-drenched Boughs

When sunlight tickles leaves so bright,
The branches groove with sheer delight.
A squirrel spins, he's on a roll,
While birds debate who has the best soul.

The laughter stirs the sleepy wood,
As critters dance, misunderstood.
A raccoon raps, so slick and fast,
While trees just shrug, 'We're meant to last.'

Wisdom in the Swaying Shadows

The whispers tease beneath the boughs,
As shadows jiggle, take a bow.
A fox remarks with clever flair,
'Life's too short! Get some fresh air!'

The owl hoots wisdom, wise and bold,
'Never mind the stories told!'
Beneath the moon's glimmering gaze,
The woods erupt in laughter's haze.

Chuckles on the Wind's Breath

The gusts carry giggles through the trees,
Rustling leaves, as light as a breeze.
A chipmunk jokes with a cheeky smile,
'Time's just a joke, so stay awhile!'

The windsconvey tales of whimsy found,
Around each twist, the laughter's loud.
Nature's quips are never bland,
They tickle hearts, a merry band.

Revelations from the Woodland Dance

In the moonlight, shadows prance,
With every move, they've got a chance.
The fireflies flash with comic flair,
'You two left feet? Don't you dare!'

Mischief flares in the peaceful night,
As woodland critters join the light.
The trees listen with patient grace,
Each joke still echoes in this space.

Playful Breezes and Feathered Calls

The wind whispers jokes to the trees,
As branches dance softly with ease.
Squirrels giggle at clouds that tease,
While birds chirp punchlines, if you please.

Sunlight flickers, playing hide and seek,
With shadows that stretch and softly peek.
Leaves rustle laughter, a gentle cheek,
In this grove where every critter's unique.

Banter Between the Gnarled Roots

Roots twist and turn like old friends teasing,
They share stories of storms, cold and freezing.
With each knot and curve, laughter's breezing,
In whispers of wood, joy is never ceasing.

Moles chime in with their own little jibe,
While beetles parade, joining the vibe.
Under the surface, there's fun to describe,
As creatures unite, nature's own tribe.

Swaying Secrets of the Scenic Grove

The trees sway gently, telling tales bold,
As sunlight dapples the stories retold.
With whispers of mischief, secrets unfold,
In a playful theater, nature's gold.

A rabbit hops in, adds a twist of fate,
Telling of carrots and dancing late.
With every rustle and soft little mate,
The scenic grove laughs, never too late.

Hilarity in the Hushed Hollow

In a hush of the hollow, where shadows gleam,
Owls wink and nod, as if in a dream.
The moonlight giggles, or so it would seem,
While critters concoct a night-time scheme.

Frogs croak a melody, all out of tune,
And fireflies twinkle in a flirtatious swoon.
With stars as their laughter, bright as the noon,
They revel in folly, beneath the round moon.

Lively Echoes in the Green Embrace

In the woods, where whispers play,
Trees shake hands at end of day.
Squirrels gossip, oh what fun,
Chasing shadows, everyone!

Leaves exchange their silly jokes,
Dancing lightly, oh how it pokes!
Branches sway as laughter flies,
Nature's humor, in disguise.

Anecdotes of the Quavering Arboreal

A twig snapped loud, what a surprise,
A rabbit jumps, and off it flies.
"Did you hear that?" an oak once said,
"Time for tea, let's raise a head!"

A bird sings high atop a branch,
While beetles prepare for a mad dance.
Every gust, a tale to weave,
With every rustle, a hearty grieve.

Whispers of the Whispering Woods

Oh, the stories those branches tell,
Of a thunderstorm and a wishing well.
A raccoon's mishap with a pie,
Left everyone laughing, oh my!

"Why do trees make such great friends?"
"Because they know how to make amends!"
With every shuffle, a secret revealed,
In every sway, laughter concealed.

Laughter in the Shivering Leaves

In a grove where pines poke fun,
Talking leaves giggle in the sun.
A busy bug with a tickle fight,
Made the whole forest laugh with delight.

They say winter can freeze the talk,
But not when the midges start to flock.
With each flutter, joy takes flight,
And the woods sing with pure delight.

Whispers in the Waving Woods

In the breeze, the trees gossip,
About squirrels and their acorns,
They chuckle at bugs dancing,
And the owl's late-night tunes.

A chipmunk slips on a branch,
As the leaves shake with laughter,
Nature's jesters, all in sync,
Creating a merry banter.

Sunlight dapples through green crowns,
While shadows play peek-a-boo,
The forest holds its breath, amazed,
By antics of a clumsy crew.

When twilight descends like a curtain,
The whispers grow into roars,
With critters sharing wild tales,
As night takes over the floors.

Laughter Beneath the Fluttering Leaves

Leaves flutter down like confetti,
Dancing to the tune of the wind,
Each landing a celebration,
Where the woodland's fun begins.

A raccoon dons a silly hat,
As the rabbits roll on the ground,
Chortles ricochet through the trunks,
A comedy show, nature-bound.

The lark cracks a joke in the air,
While toads croak in fits of mirth,
With butterflies joining the fun,
In this lively patch of earth.

Giggles echo through the boughs,
With every rustle and sway,
The woods are alive with rapture,
Where laughter is here to stay.

Jests Between the Golden Bark

Golden trunks wear a grin,
As critters exchange wisecracks,
Birds chirp about the latest news,
   Sprinklings of joy, no lack.

A deer with a crown made of leaves,
   Postures like a regal knight,
While the squirrels snicker softly,
   At the odd, playful sight.

Branches sway, their trunks tilt,
   Swinging tales of the day's play,
Every rustle a punchline,
In woodland's hilarious ballet.

As dusk drapes its cloak of humor,
   Jests float like pollen in air,
The laughter lingers in twilights,
   A forest comedy affair.

Chatter of the Shivering Canopy

Up high, the branches gossip,
Whispers of the day's delight,
A crow jokes about the rain,
While the woodpecker takes flight.

Squirrels throw nuts like confetti,
As the breeze carries their cheers,
Each thud is met with loud chuckles,
In a grove filled with playful sneers.

A sunny patch becomes the stage,
Where shadows stretch and sway,
Rabbits hop in a frolicsome line,
Dancing as if to say,

"Join us, here beneath the sky,"
As laughter weaves through each leaf,
In this vibrant, shivering space,
Where joy grows beyond belief.

Jests of the Trembling Trees

In the grove where whispers play,
The trees have jokes they sway.
One says, 'I feel a breeze,
But it's just the squirrels' tease!'

Leaves giggle as they shake,
'Is it me, or does that branch quake?'
Another chimes in with glee,
'Hold tight, or you'll spill your tea!'

A wobbly trunk pipes a tune,
'Why don't trees ever go to the moon?
They fear the lift-off and flight,
And miss the bark-tastic sight!'

Underneath, the laughter flows,
While critters join in the shows.
So next time you see a tree,
Don't shake its hand, just let it be!

Banter Beneath the Breezy Boughs

Beneath the branches, leaves discuss,
'Who's the silliest among us?'
One claims with a flutter,
'It's that clumsy bird in the gutter!'

A gust of wind joins the chat,
'Who forgot to wear a hat?'
The bark rolls its eyes with sass,
'Oh please, you've got quite the grass!'

With every sway, a punchline's hurled,
'Why did the twig feel twirled?
It wanted to be a part of the dance,
But fell flat in its own romance!'

All around, the laughter swells,
As dappled sunlight casts its spells.
These old trees know how to jest,
Underneath the skies they blessed!

Chatter Among the Shaky Stems

The stems start chatting, giggles arise,
'Look at that squirrel, he's up for a prize!'
With acorns gathered, he struts with flair,
'Then stumbles and rolls, oh how he'll despair!'

Rustling leaves join in the fun,
'Now that was a tumble, oh what a run!'
'Perhaps he should stick to the ground,
He's just too nutty for this playground!'

Two branches cross with a sly remark,
'Did you hear the tree that dreamed of the park?'
'He wanted to win the best-in-show,
But lost to a bush, and now feel so low!'

In this patch of wooden friends,
The laughter never truly ends.
With every quiver and shake,
They share stories that make the heart quake!

Chuckles in the Dancing Foliage

In the foliage where the giggles bloom,
A leaf winks as it says, 'Make room!'
For a butterfly flutters, twirls in delight,
'This is a party, oh what a sight!'

A rustling voice close by chimes in,
'I bet you can't dance, but I know I'll win!'
Grasses sway with a knowing grin,
'The real challenge is who will spin?'

Branches bow down in cheerful cheer,
'Tweety-tweets, come over here!'
And so the forest comes alive,
In this merry dance where all thrive.

From leafy laughter to earthy fun,
Even the shadows join in the run.
So next time you pass by this place,
Just listen close to the joy we embrace!

Jovial Tales from the Thicket

In a grove where the branches sway,
Squirrels gossip and dance all day.
With acorns falling, they take their chance,
To tease each other in a nutty dance.

A chipmunk tripped over a branch, it seems,
And laughed it off while dreaming dreams.
"What's the rush?" the owl turned and said,
"Just enjoy the silly while you're not dead!"

The sun was bright, a perfect affair,
A deer trained to prance, but then lost its flair.
"Don't mind me," it chuckled, "I meant to fall,
Adding more colors to spring's grand ball!"

The laughter echoes through trees that gleam,
In this jolly wood, life's a fun-filled dream.
Each critter with tales too funny to cling,
As the thicket bursts forth, let the joy take wing.

Comedic Encounters in the Arboretum

In a patch where the branches twist and twine,
A rabbit sneezed, oh what a sign!
The flowers shook, the bees flew high,
Saying, "Bless you!" from the curious sky.

A crow cracked jokes about the sun's bright hat,
"Can you believe it? It's not even flat!
With wayward rays that bring us cheer,
Let's all make shadows and disappear!"

A turtle brought snacks, but they rolled away,
"Who knew a picnic could turn into play?"
The squirrels all cheered, with their teeth in the pie,
While the turtle just sighed, "I'll bake a new try."

In this garden of giggles, the laughter runs wild,
Nature's own theater, where everyone smiled.
With every small mishap, a new tale begins,
In comedic encounters, the joy always wins.

Joyful Exchanges in the Jagged Roots

Beneath gnarled roots, where secrets reside,
The hedgehog and fox shared a cozy side.
"Tell me your tales, but keep them neat,
I can't handle snacks that are bittersweet!"

A raccoon popped in, with a sparkle in eye,
"I found a sock! But shh, don't ask why.
It danced away, with a life of its own,
Now I'm the king of a sock puppet throne!"

A badger chimed in with a riddle so sly,
"What's orange, has whiskers, and likes to fly?"
"We don't quite know," said the fox with a grin,
"Perhaps it's your cousin, come out for a spin!"

Amid the old roots, their laughter grew loud,
As the woodland rejoiced, a very fine crowd.
In joyful exchanges, they crafted a scene,
Of quirky companions, all living the dream.

Smiles in the Silvered Glade

In the silvered glade, leaves chatter and sway,
A squirrel trips, oh what a ballet!
With acorns dropped, a nutty parade,
Laughter echoes, in sunlight displayed.

A deer prances by with a curious glance,
She steps on a twig, oh what a mischance!
The forest erupts in a fit of delight,
As critters join in, they dance through the light.

A rabbit winks, sporting a cap,
While owls hold court in their evening nap.
Each rustle and giggle proves nature's jest,
In every heart, a little laugh rests.

So come take a stroll through this joyful place,
Where every critter wears a smile on its face.
Under branches that sway, in the bright sunny glade,
We find in the forest, the fun that we've made.

Friendly Teasing in the Timberline

At the timberline, the pines stand tall,
With whispers of laughter as leaves gently fall.
A chipmunk brags of his mountain high race,
Only to trip, and fall flat on his face!

The tall trees chuckle, their limbs all a-shake,
As the chipmunk dusts off, for pride's own sake.
"Next time, my friend, try to mind your feet!"
Comes the gentle teasing—oh, isn't it sweet?

A fox sneaks around, playing hide and seek,
She leaps to surprise, but gives quite a squeak.
"Too loud to be sneaky!" a wise doe declares,
As the forest erupts in a chorus of glares.

With shadows that dance, and the sun on the rise,
The friends share their jests under wide open skies.
In this tender wood, where laughter resides,
The magic of mischief, the warm-hearted guides.

Breezy Jests of the Green Giants

Among giants of green, the breeze carries jokes,
As vines intertwine like the finest of cloaks.
A parrot squawks tales of mischief anew,
While ants whisper secrets where few ever knew.

A bear takes a dip in the cool, crystal stream,
Only to find that he's lost his old dream.
With a splash and a snort, he emerges all wet,
"Oh, who needs a fish? I'll dry off, you bet!"

The wind plays a tune that tickles the leaves,
As shadows weave stories of tricksters and thieves.
A raccoon peeks out, with a grin on his face,
In this land of tall trees, there's always a space.

So gather around for a chuckle or two,
In the heart of the woods where the humor is true.
With each rustle and gust, joy takes to the skies,
In this glorious glade, we all share the ties.

Humor in the Flickering Shade

In the flickering shade, the grass softly laughs,
As shadows of creatures play playful crafts.
A turtle, slow-moving, makes quite the scene,
Says, "Life's not a race, I'm just keeping it green!"

A fly lands with flair on a pebble so round,
While crickets debate on the best final sound.
"Your chirp needs some work!" an old frog croaks out,
"Just sing from your heart, that's what it's about!"

The sun dips low, as shadows grow long,
With quips exchanged softly, like nature's own song.
As the world gently hushes under evening's embrace,
These moments together, we gladly embrace.

So dance in the dusk, let your spirits take flight,
For laughter is nature's own soft, glowing light.
In the flickering shade where all creatures abide,
We cherish the humor that twirls at our side.

Glee in the Dancing Sunbeams

In a field where sunbeams play,
The flowers giggle in bright array.
A ladybug wears a tiny crown,
While ants parade in a wiggly gown.

The grass blades sway with jokes to share,
Tickling the toes of passers there.
A butterfly flutters, gives a wink,
And all the world stops just to think.

A squirrel hops with acorn cheer,
Shouting 'Catch me if you dare, my dear!'
With each leap and bound, the laughter lifts,
Nature's canvas painted with sweet gifts.

So let the sunshine warm your soul,
As laughter dances, making you whole.
In this joyous, bright spree we find,
The merriment of every kind.

Harmony Among the Swaying Sentinels

Under the watch of trees so tall,
Their whispers tickle, make us sprawl.
A woodpecker drums a silly beat,
As squirrels engage in playful feat.

Branches sway like carefree dancers,
In the breeze, they find their chances.
A chipmunk struts in tiny shoes,
While the world laughs, sharing views.

Leaves are confetti in the air,
As nature throws a wild affair.
In every rustle and gentle sway,
A new adventure starts the day.

The sun dips low, in colors bright,
The trees exchange their quirks with delight.
In this grove where laughter flows,
Friendship blooms where the green grass grows.

Tidbits of Joy in the Whispering Trees

In the forest where secrets hide,
The trees chuckle, swaying wide.
Funny faces in their bark,
With tales that light the evening dark.

A bunny hops with a twitching nose,
Chasing the tickles from the rose.
A deer poses with a silly grin,
As the sun dips low, the magic begins.

Birds exchange puns, do a flip,
While foxes plan a dinner trip.
Every breeze carries a giggly tone,
In this realm, we're never alone.

So whisper back to those who sway,
Share your laughter, come what may.
In the trees where joy is shared,
Life's little quirks are truly bared.

Riddles Among the Leafy Giants

Beneath the giants with leaves so wide,
Mischief brews where shadows hide.
An owl hoots riddles, wise and bold,
While the young ones giggle at stories told.

A raccoon dons a mask of cheer,
Saying, 'Who's sneaky? Come here, come near!'
With swaying branches, they shake and tease,
Inventing games with delightful ease.

Breezes whisper playful rhymes,
In the arms of nature, it's always fun times.
A gentle sway, a twirl of delight,
The leafy giants dance through the night.

At dusk, when the world feels light and snug,
Joy fills the air like a warm, soft hug.
In their laughter, we find our way,
Among the secrets of nature's play.

Jokes of the Rustling Canopy

Why did the leaf blush so bright?
It saw the bark's joke, quite a sight!
The branches chuckled, oh so loud,
While the roots giggled, feeling proud.

A squirrel slipped on a slick, wet bark,
Said, "Now that's how you make your mark!"
The wind howled back with a whispery tease,
"You're the clumsiest critter among the trees!"

A wise owl hooted late at night,
"I know why the trees dance with delight."
They told a pun that made them shake,
'Life's a hoot, for goodness' sake!'

The pinecones nodded, green in the glow,
Laughing at pine trees, putting on a show.
When trees tell tales around twilight's glow,
Their humor sprinkles joy, leaves in tow.

Giggling in the Golden Grove

In the grove where laughter paints the air,
A rabbit joked, unaware of a dare.
"Have you heard about the shy little sprout?"
"It only laughs when the sun is out!"

The sunbeams winked, rolling with glee,
As a lizard chimed in, 'come dance with me!'
Caterpillars wriggled, trying to sway,
While butterflies laughed, 'Don't fade away!'

A bumblebee buzzed with a grin so wide,
"I've pollen, it's humor, let's take a ride!"
With wings like ribbons they fluttered about,
Chasing giggles and whispers, no doubt!

Oh, in this grove, there's folly galore,
As crickets chirp jokes from door to door.
And when the moon shines, hear the big oak boast,
"I'm the funniest tree that you'll ever toast!"

Mirth Among the Fluttering Fronds

In the ferns where the giggles blend,
The grasshoppers hop, their antics extend.
With every jump, a quip they'll fling,
'The bugs are in charge, let the laughter ring!'

A butterfly teased with a twirl and sway,
"Don't leaf me hanging, come out to play!"
The beetles chuckled, all in a line,
"We're the best dancers, can you outshine?"

The shy fox snickered, watching in awe,
As the snails took the stage, without a flaw.
"Their shells are like trophies, so strong and bright!"
Bet you didn't see that coming tonight!

In the shadows where the echoes shimmer,
Laughter sparkles, making hearts glimmer.
So join in the fun, let the fronds have their say,
In the whimsical world, where humor won't stray!

Sprightly Murmurs of the Woodland

In the woodland whispers, the stories collide,
With every rustle, secrets slide.
The chipmunks chattered, quick on their feet,
"Did you hear the one about the fish and the beet?"

A deer made a joke about grass so long,
"Why do bugs think they all belong?"
The trees shook with laughter, branches aglow,
"Because they're all rooted in high-spirited flow!"

As shadows danced in a flickering show,
The toads recited old songs from below.
"Do toes really tickle when you jump for fun?"
They exchanged many grins while making a run!

And as twilight came with its blanket of stars,
The owls hooted freely, sharing their bars.
In the sprightly woods, where mirth is found,
Laughter rings true, nature's joyful sound.

Treetop Twinkles of Humor

In the breeze, a leaf does dance,
Whispering jokes, taking a chance.
A squirrel laughs, his cheeks all full,
He hoards his nuts; is he quite the fool?

The sun beams down, a golden ray,
Tickling branches in a playful sway.
A bird sings tunes of silly delight,
While shadows prance, hiding in flight.

The mountains giggle, their peaks so steep,
Echoing laughter, that stirs us from sleep.
A wind chime jangles a merry tune,
As the trees chuckle, beneath the moon.

Nature's jesters, with roots so tight,
Joke around 'til the fall of night.
Oh, join the fun in this leafy plot,
Where every giggle is a sweet little thought.

Nature's Gadabout Glee

A rabbit races, quick as a thought,
Chasing his tail like a prankster caught.
The flowers giggle, their petals aglow,
Poking fun at the bees buzzing low.

The brook babbles secrets, swift as a hare,
Echoing laughter that's light as air.
A fox in the shade, with a smirk on his face,
Claims to know every last sunbeam's place.

The sun dresses trees in a golden hue,
While shadows play tag, not caring what's due.
The chipmunk shares tales of his daring flight,
Spinning yarns in the warm, waning light.

Each critter joins in, a whimsical scene,
In nature's wild banter, where all is serene.
Laughter spills out, like rain from the sky,
Bubbling with joy, as the moments drift by.

Amusing Secrets of the Swaying Branches

The willows whisper, soft and spry,
Sharing giggles as clouds drift by.
A playful breeze, a branch does tease,
With secrets of nature, shared with ease.

A raccoon's sly grin, nocturnal delight,
Sneaks through the thicket, a comical sight.
While owls chuckle in wise, muted tones,
Swaying along with the evening's moans.

Each acorn drops like a punchline clear,
Tickling the ground, what a hoot to hear!
The trees sway low, a comedic ballet,
As nature's jesters make merry today.

In this lively world of fluttering glee,
Laughter and whimsy roam wild and free.
Nature's own stand-up, a splendid array,
Where every turn brings a light-hearted play.

Lighthearted Conversations of the Canopy

As pine needles chatter in windswept cheer,
They branch out stories for all who are near.
A woodpecker drums out a comical beat,
While the sunlight giggles, skipping down street.

Beneath a stout oak, sits a wise old sage,
With leaves that rustle like turning a page.
He snickers at critters scurrying along,
He knows all the tales of the brave and the wrong.

Clouds drift by, wearing silly hats,
Drawing doodles of friendly cats.
The meadow grins as daisies twirl,
In the joyous dance of the world's sweet whirl.

Nature's own forum, with laughter abound,
Echoes in hearts, where merriment's found.
So listen and laugh, take a moment to ponder,
In this canopy laughter, let your spirits wander.

Frolicsome Rhythms of Nature's Stage

In the breeze the leaves do dance,
With whispers soft, they take a chance.
A squirrel prances, leaps with glee,
While birds exchange their jokes, you see.

The branches sway like arms in cheer,
As if they share a secret, dear.
A rabbit hops with playful flair,
And shakes its tail, high in the air.

The shadows play a game of hide,
While sunlight giggles, warm and wide.
All around, the laughter grows,
As nature puts on quite a show.

So join this merry, wild parade,
Where every chuckle won't soon fade.
A symphony of fun, no doubt,
In this grand green, a joyful rout.

Revelry in the Shaking Canopy

The trees converse in rustling tones,
With jokes exchanged in leafy zones.
As winds take hold, a playful shake,
The branches laugh, no heart can break.

Oh, how the sunbeams play and tease,
They slip and slide with such great ease.
A chipmunk jokes, then darts away,
While flowers giggle in bright array.

The sky above rolls clouds of fluff,
While nature's banter is warm and rough.
A playful breeze, a hidden wink,
And all around, there's time to think.

So join the fun beneath the leaves,
Where laughter flows, and joy believes.
In every crackle, every sway,
Nature's humor leads the way.

Musings in the Mellow Breeze

The wind whispers sweet nothings loud,
It tells a tale to every crowd.
A butterfly flutters in retreat,
While daisies giggle and tap their feet.

A fox trots by with a knowing glance,
It's not just chance—it's nature's dance.
The brook behind sings silly songs,
While crickets chirp where humor belongs.

The clouds above play peek-a-boo,
As sunshine spills a golden hue.
A sleepy dog rolls on the grass,
While shadows throw a lively pass.

So linger here, breathe in the fun,
Under the gaze of the glowing sun.
Let nature's chuckle fill your heart,
And in this joy, you'll find your part.

Contents of a Windy Laugh

The wind arrives with a hearty jest,
Tickling leaves and causing unrest.
A crow caws out with comedic flair,
As nature's audience stops to stare.

Beneath the boughs, laughter echoes wide,
As squirrels jump and take a ride.
A turtle pokes its head out slow,
With puns that only birds would know.

The shadows stretch, the sunlight beams,
While branches sway, like playful dreams.
A bee buzzes in a silly spree,
Just buzzing by, as happy as can be.

Join in the fun, let your heart grow,
In this treehouse of joy, let laughter flow.
For in every rustle, in every laugh,
Nature's joke is a heartfelt craft.

Nectar of Laughter in the Aspen Thicket

In the grove where branches sway,
The trees tell jokes by light of day.
A squirrel laughs at its own wit,
   Dropping acorns—what a hit!

Leaves giggle in the gentle breeze,
Whispering secrets with such ease.
The bark's got puns, it's plain to see,
   Nature's stand-up, wild and free.

Beneath the canopy's bright delight,
Roots converse in the moonlight bright.
A raccoon's chuckle, a fox's grin,
   Join the fun—let's all join in!

With every rustle and playful twist,
The forest's humor can't be missed.
Come one, come all, take a seat,
   Nature's comedy is quite the treat!

Tales of Tickled Trunks

Tickled trunks in a dancing line,
Sharing giggles with a twist of vine.
Each ring a story, each bend a laugh,
Nature's humor carved in half.

A woodpecker's tap, a drumming beat,
Frames the rhythm of laughter sweet.
The caterpillars, in silly hats,
Join the fun—imagine that!

Breeze brings jokes from distant lands,
Whirled with whispers, planters' hands.
"Knock knock!" calls a blushing sprout,
Responsibilities? What's that about?

In the woods where joy is found,
Rooted laughter shakes the ground.
So share a grin with those you meet,
And join the trunks in their heartbeat!

Chime of the Cascading Leaves

Leaves are laughing, their colors bright,
Tickling the air from morning to night.
Each flutter a chuckle, a bright confound,
In the lively dance where joy is found.

With every gust, a tale unfolds,
Of playful breezes and mischief bold.
Saplings tease, the elders chuckle,
Beneath their branches, we all huddle.

A fox prances, in humorous haste,
With antics that never go to waste.
The stream sings back with a bubbly grin,
Nature's laughter welcomes all in.

Oh, hear the chime of the leaves above,
Whispering secrets, wrapped in love.
A giddy whirl through branches new,
Where silliness blossoms, and dreams come true!

Gleeful Darting Among the Branches

In joyful leaps, the critters bound,
Through branches high, they spin around.
A sparrow chirps with a comic flair,
As acorns tumble through the air.

Here comes a rabbit, quick and spry,
Chasing shadows as they fly.
With each twist, a new delight,
Zooming past, what a silly sight!

The chipmunks chatter with glee and wit,
Racing each other—who will admit?
That laughter ripples through the trees,
A banquet of joy on the gentle breeze.

So join the dance, don't hesitate,
In nature's play, let's celebrate.
With every rustle and merry dive,
We weave the joy that keeps us alive!

Whimsical Whispers of the Wilderness

In the breeze, the trees conspire,
Leaves giggle, dancing with desire.
A squirrel juggles acorns with a flair,
While rabbits plot mischief without a care.

The sun winks down, a playful tease,
While chipmunks chatter, buzzing like bees.
A woodpecker knocks upon a tree,
Saying, "Who's laughing? Come join me!"

Breezy banter fills the air,
Foxes prance with delightful flair.
Nature's jesters, oh what a show,
In every rustle, a chuckle will flow.

So take a stroll through this merry land,
Where even the shadows have laughter planned.
Fluffy clouds up above our heads,
Join the silly symphony, where joy spreads.

The Smiles of Evergreen Friends

Pines poke their heads, act quite aloof,
While ferns whisper secrets, under the roof.
A shy little owl hoots in the night,
Cracking jokes that give stars a fright.

The brook giggles, splashing its glee,
As turtles play tag, bold as can be.
An old badger grins under his scruff,
Saying, "Life's too short, let's not bluff!"

Twilight winks, a playful jest,
Fireflies flicker, dancing their best.
With every shimmer, smiles take flight,
Creating a canvas of joy in the night.

The moss carpets softly the weary ground,
Cushions of laughter wherever we're found.
Join this affable gathering at play,
Where smiles grow wild, come what may.

Gleeful Giggles of the Glade

In the glade, laughter rings bright,
Where shadows and sunlight weave pure delight.
A family of deer in playful parade,
Casting long shadows in this sunny glade.

Bunnies hop high, chasing their tails,
While ladybugs juggle, defying the trails.
An acorn drops with a thud and a bounce,
Causing a ruckus that makes us all flounce.

With laughter so rich, it fills up the air,
As birds chirp tunes without any care.
The mushrooms chuckle, proud of their spots,
Giving a nod to the fanciful thoughts.

As twilight approaches, the giggles still soar,
With whispers of joy, always wanting more.
Nature's own jesters, let's dance with delight,
In the heart of the glade, everything feels right.

Elysian Echoes of the Arboreal

In the canopy high, the crows caw with cheer,
While owls make quips that we all want to hear.
The dappled sunlight plays peek-a-boo,
As butterflies flit like they have something to do.

Down below, the puddles reflect up their grins,
While frogs strike a pose as they practice their spins.
The mossy logs share their tales so grand,
Filling the air with fun and a band.

Whimsical wonders ripple like streams,
As critters all gather, fulfilling their dreams.
With laughter abundant in this fanciful realm,
Nature's brigade keeps joy at the helm.

So skip through the boughs, on this whimsical ride,
Where the echoes of laughter and trees coincide.
In every green leaf, and soft rustle found,
Elysian tales of joy are unbound.

Conversations in the Calm

In the forest, whispers play,
Leaves chuckle, night turns to day.
A squirrel scolds a tree so tall,
"Stop dropping acorns, it's not a ball!"

The brook bubbles, laughs a tune,
Echoes dance beneath the moon.
A hare hops by, with ears so spry,
"Do you hear that? It's a butterfly!"

Breezes giggle as they sway,
With tales of mischief on display.
An owl hoots, in playful jest,
"Who's the wisest? Let's contest!"

In this glade, joy's forever,
Nature's humor, by any measure.
So join the fun, let laughter flow,
In these woods, all spirits glow.

The Dance of Mirthful Breezes

Breezes waltz in the starlit night,
Twisting leaves, oh what a sight!
A chipmunk spins, with wild delight,
"Catch me if you can!"—what a flight!

The moon grins down, a mischievous friend,
Catching shadows that twist and bend.
A fox in stripes gives a little shout,
"I'm fancy, don't you dare doubt!"

Blades of grass giggle along,
Nature hums a cheeky song.
The nightingale joins in with flair,
"Let's have a fiesta, if you dare!"

Together they twirl to the cosmic beat,
While stars wink down, oh what a treat!
In every twist, find joy and cheer,
As laughter echoes, crystal clear.

Fables of the Flickering Glimpse

Flickers of light weave through the trees,
Tales of mischief ride the breeze.
A raccoon grins as it sneaks a snack,
"Who left this treat? I'll take a crack!"

Whispers of fables flutter near,
In this wild woods, never fear.
The lightning bugs play hide and seek,
"Catch me, quick! I'm not that meek!"

Tales of whispers and playful sighs,
Chirping crickets and owl's wise eyes.
A grandma tree shakes her leafy head,
"Remember, my dears, this is how we're fed!"

Every flicker holds a grin,
Nature's wisdom, let's dive in!
Stories mingle beneath the glow,
In this realm, let laughter flow.

The Harmony of Hoots and Howls

Amid the echoes of starlit calls,
Howls and hoots fill the night with thralls.
An owl quips, "Who's your evening friend?"
A coyote laughs, "Let the games transcend!"

The bushes rustle, secrets shared,
With every sound, the wild is bared.
An antlered deer prances, full of chat,
"Come join us too, don't sit on that!"

In this theater of nature's merry show,
Laughter erupts, oh how it flows!
The moon sparkles, a radiant key,
Unlocking joy in harmony.

Every creature shares a song,
Under the stars, where we belong.
Together we dance, howl, and hoot,
In this lively forest, take root!

Banter Along the Breezy Trail

The trees are whispering jokes with glee,
Swaying in rhythm, so carefree.
Squirrels chuckle, sharing a nut,
While rabbits trip over their own strut.

A crow caws loudly, adds to the jest,
As leaves fall down, nature's best fest.
The breeze carries laughter, sweet and bright,
As sunlight dances, igniting delight.

Mice gossip softly, all in a row,
Trading tales of the farmer's scarecrow.
The path is alive with chuckles and prance,
Who knew the woods held such a dance?

Nature's humor plays on repeat,
Even the rocks have a witty seat.
We're all just players in this merry play,
On a banter-filled stroll, come laugh away.

Smiles in the Silver Light

Under the moon, the crickets sing,
Did you hear what the fireflies did bring?
They flashed their lights in a quirky bout,
And tangled the owls, oh what a shout!

The shadows skip, as if in jest,
Chasing each other, they never rest.
A fox tells tales that twist and twine,
As stars wink down, saying, "Look, it's fine!"

A deer pranks a rabbit with a quick hop,
Makes it jump high, then starts to stop.
Together they giggle under the bright sky,
In the silver light, spirits fly high.

Each moment a jest, a sparkle, a theme,
In this nighttime carnival, we all beam.
With laughter the best, our worries take flight,
In the dance of the forest, smiles feel just right.

Echoes of Joy Through the Trembling Branches

Beneath the boughs where laughter flows,
The trees high-five, or so it goes.
A chipmunk chats with a wise old owl,
Sharing secrets with a mischievous scowl.

Branches giggle, swaying to tune,
Setting the stage for a comedy boon.
A squirrel drops acorns, a funny old trick,
While nearby, a raccoon plays hide-and-snick.

The wind sends echoes that tickle and tease,
A game of tag, it brings to its knees.
All creatures join in, a whimsical band,
Creating joy in this leafy land.

As shadows dance with humor untold,
Nature's laughter is worth more than gold.
From tree to tree, the echoes do sing,
A joyful crescendo that makes our hearts spring.

Mirth Beneath the Dancing Foliage

Beneath the leaves, there's a party on ground,
Where laughter and joy are utterly crown'd.
A hedgehog cracks jokes, spiky yet sweet,
While badgers bring snacks for the merry feast.

The foliage rustles, it cannot contain,
The chuckling and grinning, a jovial gain.
A turtle spins tales, though it's slow as can be,
While butterflies flutter, all fancy and free.

Each twig holds a secret, a pun, or a jest,
In this whimsical place, we're all truly blessed.
With every soft breeze, we lift our hearts high,
Finding joy in the rustling, the dance of the sky.

So come join the laughter, beneath boughs so wide,
Where mirth is abundant, and shadows collide.
Together we flourish, in giggles and gleam,
In the embrace of the woods, we craft our dream.

Laughing with the Fluttering Flora

In the breeze, the leaves do sway,
Whisper secrets, come what may.
Bunnies hop, with ears so tall,
They hear the chuckles, one and all.

Squirrels dance on branches high,
Dropping acorns from the sky.
The flowers giggle, colors bright,
Beneath the sun, they feel just right.

A ladybug with spots so neat,
Hitches rides on tiny feet.
They all chuckle, what a sight,
Nature's antics bring pure delight.

With every rustle, laughter spreads,
A chorus of joy in leafy beds.
As butterflies whirl in playful flight,
They add their laughter, pure and light.

Serenades of the Shaking Stand

Up in the branches, whispers play,
Birds crack jokes for the light of day.
The owls hoot with wisdom old,
While young saplings bravely bold.

A bumblebee buzzes, quite the tease,
Stealing nectar with expert ease.
The petals blush, not just for show,
As bees spin tales, they come and go.

A tree trunk leans, playing the fool,
Trying to stay upright, it's a duel.
The roots chuckle, firm and wise,
As leaves spin tales beneath the skies.

With every gust, the chorus swells,
Nature's laughter, ringing bells.
In this grove, where giggles grow,
Every leaf tells tales we know.

Merriment in the Mystical Grove

In dappled light, the shadows dance,
The ferns flirt, given half a chance.
Mushrooms giggle, sprouting sly,
Chasing clouds in the sky so high.

Worms in suits, all dressed in dirt,
Swapping stories with a twirl and flirt.
Ladybugs laugh, with a wink and grin,
Creating tales where fun begins.

The wind plays tricks, a breezy friend,
Swirling leaves that twist and bend.
If you listen close, you may just hear,
The sound of laughter, always near.

A squirrel tries to climb a tree,
Dressed in acorns, wild and free.
With every stumble, the groves ignite,
A symphony of joy, pure delight.

The Amusing Path of the Rustling Understory

Along the path where shadows peek,
Skunks in tuxedos play hide and seek.
With every rustle, giggles grow,
A parade of critters steals the show.

Mice don hats made of wildflower crowns,
While raccoons throw their tiny gowns.
Sassy skinks take center stage,
Every creature turns a page.

Beneath the leafy canopies,
Chirping crickets coax the breeze.
Frogs wear tuxedos, leaping proud,
In the backdrop, nature's lively crowd.

Each step along this cheerful trail,
Echoes laughter, a joyous hail.
With every turn, more laughter springs,
In the understory, fun's the king.

Whimsies of the Woodland Breeze

Beneath the sway of branches fair,
Squirrels chatter without a care.
"Is that a nut or just a stone?"
Nature's jesters, all alone.

A rabbit hops with quite a flair,
"Why not dance? I'm light as air!"
While butterflies flit without a clue,
Their silent giggles drift like dew.

The windy whispers tease the trees,
"Hold on tight, it's quite the breeze!"
A fox runs by in a somersault,
"This woodland life is quite the vault!"

When shadows lengthen, and stars ignite,
The fireflies blink with sheer delight.
"Can you catch me?" they seem to say,
As laughter echoes till break of day.

The Symposium of the Shivering Leaves

In rustling tones, the leaves conspire,
"What's your secret? What's your fire?"
One rustles back, "It's just the sun,
But shade's where all the cool is done!"

The breeze joins in, a playful prank,
"What's the plan? Let's fill the bank!"
A pinecone chimes, "I'm rolling free!"
"Get it, rolling? Join with me!"

A woodpecker's drum creates a beat,
"This gathering's quite the cheerful treat!"
As deer prance through, they wink and say,
"Hurry up, or you'll miss the play!"

With every gust, a tale unfolds,
Of whispered dreams and secrets told.
Mother Nature laughs, drops her veil,
"Keep it light, let laughter sail!"

Nurtured Cheers of the Nature's Children

Twigs snap underfoot in glee,
"Did you hear that? It's quite a spree!"
A colony of ants march in line,
"Join us now! It's snack time!"

A chatty bluebird starts to sing,
"Gather 'round for tales of spring!"
While chipmunks pause for a sweet tease,
"Fast as lightning, eat your peas!"

The brook babbles jokes, splashes joy,
"Why so serious? Come on, oh boy!"
As frogs join in with a croaky cheer,
"Splash a little, no need to fear!"

Beneath the boughs, laughter rises,
Nature's stage is full of surprises.
In every corner of the wood,
Laughter thrives, all's understood.

Enjoying the Cascade of Color

Leaves turn red like jokes, so bold,
"What's the punchline? Come share, behold!"
A golden hue sways in the light,
"Is it fall? No, it's pure delight!"

Fall's comedian, the pumpkin, sings,
"Orange you glad for all these things?"
While acorns drop with playful cheers,
"Catch us quick! We're worth your years!"

The tangy scent of cider fills,
"Let's toast to autumn's gentle thrills!"
As laughter dances through the scene,
"Who knew nature could be so keen!"

In vibrant paths, the joy cascades,
Every moment, like sunlight, parades.
With colors bold, and silly sights,
Nature's jokes are pure delights!

Tales Told by the Trees

In the breeze, the leaves discuss,
How squirrels dance, and not make a fuss.
One whispers tales of a windy snore,
While others giggle, "Oh, please, not more!"

An old oak brags of his sturdy stance,
Claiming he once led a lumberyard dance.
But the birch just laughs with a rustle so sweet,
"You were just tripped by a clown on his feet!"

Frivolous Flights Among the Foliage

A feathered friend did stumble and fall,
Claimed he was flying, but missed the call.
The branches chuckled, swayed to and fro,
As the robin blushed in a fiery glow.

Squirrels raced, tails twitched like a joke,
« We're the funniest critters, no need to provoke! »
Yet a wise old crow cackled with glee,
« You're not as amusing as you think you be! »

Laugh Lines on the Bark

The bark, it wrinkles with laughter anew,
Each groove a giggle, a joke just for you.
A tree with a grin holds a secret within,
'Twas a beetle that tickled his skin with a spin!

"I toppled a tree!" yelled a boastful pine,
But the aspen chimed in, "Oh darling, you whine!
It was merely a leaf that slipped on the floor,
And you fell, my friend, avoiding a bore!"

A Chorus of Friendly Chortles

From the canopy high, a laughter rang loud,
As the willows swayed, drawing in the crowd.
"Do you think we're tall just to show off our flair?"
"Or is it the chatter we share in the air?"

As the breeze carried tales of jest and of cheer,
The trunks lined up closer to lend a small ear.
"Let's gather 'round, dear friends, share a joke,
For it's always refreshing to laugh 'til we choke!"

Folly of the Flitting Sparrows

Sparrows dance on twigs so fine,
Chasing crumbs and dreams divine.
They hop and flap with chirps so loud,
Imitating the breeze, feeling proud.

One lands with grace, a comic sight,
Stumbles, fluffs, and takes off in flight.
With every gust, they twist and twirl,
Nature's own feathery whirl-a-girl.

Amidst the trees, they chat with glee,
Sharing secrets like old sea.
In laughter's echoes, they play and tease,
Making merry in the golden leaves.

Oh, the folly of these sprightly friends,
Their jests abuzz as the daylight bends.
With leaves a-shiver, they leap and dive,
In the funny ballet, they feel alive.

Jestful Shadows on Sunlit Trails

On trails where shadows prance and play,
Laughter echoes the light of day.
Leaves chuckle as the sunbeams chase,
While creatures skitter and quicken their pace.

A toad hops along on a wooden path,
Partaking in nature's silly math.
As squirrels race in their acorn heist,
Each wiggle brings giggles, oh, how nice!

The sun dips low, leaving playful marks,
Where shadows whisper, sharing sparks.
In jestful sways of branches and boughs,
The world erupts in spontaneous yows!

Oh, to be lost in the chuckles around,
As mirthful echoes abound, abound!
With every step, new jokes unfold,
Nature's comedy, brash and bold.

The Joy of Connected Canopies

Look up high, where treetops meet,
In a canopy that's hard to beat.
Branches wobble in friendly jest,
Underneath, the critters rest.

A squirrel yells, 'Jump over here!'
While birds hum tunes both bright and clear.
With branches linked, they form a crowd,
Shouting jokes, both silly and loud.

Oh, how the breezes carry their laughter,
Echoing through the green, ever after.
Each rustle and sway brings giggles anew,
In their lofty play, an amusing view.

From whispering leaves to beckoning skies,
Connected canopies know no goodbyes.
Under their watch, the world's a jest,
In nature's embrace, we're truly blessed.

Delights in the Dappled Light

In dappled light where shadows dance,
The trees engage in a leafy prance.
Spotting critters in playful plight,
With chuckling whispers, oh what a sight!

A chipmunk munches, a goofy grin,
With every bite, it's a giggle within.
The sun peek-a-boos through the leafy stands,
Lighting up laughter across the lands.

As day unfolds, the antics commence,
With rustling leaves, all feel the suspense.
Squirrels jump high, like jesters in the air,
Chasing the shadows without a care.

In this realm of wonder, glee takes flight,
Delights abound in the dappled light.
With each rustle, a tale is spun,
In the joy of nature, we all are one.

Camaraderie in the Crooked Trail

The trees giggle as they sway,
Making faces, come what may.
Branches waving, roots in jest,
Nature's friends, they love the quest.

Squirrels play tag in the green,
Chasing shadows, fast and keen.
A deer trips over a stone,
Laughter echoes - you're not alone.

Birds chirp puns in the bright sun,
Their merry song is full of fun.
While flowers stick out their tongues,
In this place where joy belongs.

Every footstep stirs a cheer,
The crooked path brings friends near.
Through this woodland, spirits lift,
In this dance, we share a gift.

Lighthearted Laughter of the Leaves

Leaves chatter softly on the breeze,
Tickling branches like a tease.
Whispered jokes from bark to bark,
The forest sparkles with its lark.

Mice play tricks on hasty frogs,
Sneaky pranks among the logs.
A breeze swings low, a feathered jest,
In this mirth, we find our rest.

Sunbeams tickle every face,
In nature's laughter, we find grace.
Each rustling leaf, a comic coin,
In this grove where friends conjoin.

Joy blooms bright in every nook,
As nature shares its playful book.
In the dance of every tree,
Laughter lives eternally.

Jovial Reflections in the Forest Floor

Toadstools giggle as they grow,
Poking fun at shadows low.
In the mist, a rabbit grins,
The forest knows where fun begins.

Mushrooms wear their caps askew,
Fashion statements, just for you.
A winding path sprinkled with cheer,
Echoes laughter, far and near.

Frogs croak jokes in a sly way,
Croaking laughter, day by day.
Squirrels toss their nuts around,
In this glory, joy is found.

A playful breeze runs through the pines,
Telling tales like aged wines.
In every nook, friendship grows,
Nature's humor ever flows.

Revels of the Rustling Understory

Beneath the trees, a secret dance,
Frogs in tuxedos take a chance.
They leap for joy, they leap for fun,
The woodland ball has just begun.

Ants with top hats march in line,
Bearing crumbs like jewels that shine.
While ladybugs put on a show,
In mirrored leaves, their colors glow.

Every twig plays piano notes,
The forest choir softly gloats.
In shadows deep, the laughter swells,
Each rustling leaf, a tale it tells.

Breezy whispers fill the air,
In this revel, friends lay bare.
With every rustle, joy restores,
The forest floor, where friendship soars.

Chuckles Through the Swaying Branches

The trees are laughing all around,
Their leaves like chatter, a cheerful sound.
A squirrel slips, he takes a dive,
And all the branches seem to jive.

The brook joins in with a bubbly glee,
Tickling the rocks, a melody.
The wind plays games, a playful tease,
Whirling the twigs with graceful ease.

A bug in shades gives a grand parade,
While shadows dance in light's cascade.
The mossy floor erupts in jig,
As laughter echoes, bold and big.

They say the forest holds secrets tight,
But here, it's jokes that take to flight.
With every breeze, a punchline near,
In this wild space, joy's crystal clear.

Lighthearted Whispers of the Wild

In twilight's glow, the crickets sing,
Their symphony of chirps, such a zing!
The fireflies wink, a bright surprise,
As laughter dances in their eyes.

A rabbit hops, a gallant knight,
Claiming his patch in the fading light.
The breeze whispers secrets of glee,
As nature hums in harmony.

A turtle slow with a humorous pout,
Mocks the hare's fast and furious route.
Branches sway, their jokes quite spry,
A gentle breeze, a giggle, a sigh.

When night falls down like a fluffy cap,
The stars join in for a cheerful clap.
Each rustle and stir, a whimsical thread,
In this wild tapestry, laughter's widespread.

Revelry in the Ruffling Thicket

The thicket buzzes with jolly jests,
While critters trade their grander quests.
A chipmunk claims his acorn throne,
With jokes so loud, they can't be loaned.

The thorns shake hands, a tangled cheer,
To share some giggles, far and near.
With each rustle, they exchange a jest,
In this fun realm, they never rest.

The backdrop hums, a playful tone,
As flowers sway like laughter blown.
A curious fox in a silly guise,
Dances under wide-open skies.

When the sun dips low, the laughter peaks,
With every sound, the thicket speaks.
So gather 'round, let the stories flow,
In this merry patch, let good vibes grow.

Merry Murmurs of Nature's Chorus

In sun-kissed glades where the shadows play,
Nature sings its light-hearted way.
A bunny thumps with a comedic flair,
While daisies sway with cheerful air.

The bluebirds joke about the sky,
Chasing clouds as they flutter by.
With every chirp, they weave a tune,
That tickles the heart, like a warm afternoon.

A dapper deer struts with pride,
In shades of brown, the forest his guide.
With every step, a wink, a grin,
As laughter fills the woodlands in.

So join the chorus, let laughter soar,
Among the trees, forevermore.
In every rustle, a joke to hear,
Nature's humor crystal clear.

www.ingramcontent.com/pod-product-compliance
Lightning Source LLC
Chambersburg PA
CBHW071829160426
43209CB00003B/249